Tracing Our GERMAN Roots

LEDA SILVER

John Muir Publications
Santa Fe, New Mexico

Acknowledgments
To librarians. They make magic.

John Muir Publications, P.O. Box 613, Santa Fe, New Mexico 87504
© 1994 by John Muir Publications
All rights reserved. Published 1994
Printed in the United States of America

First edition. First printing February 1994
        First TWG printing February 1994

Library of Congress Cataloging-in-Publication Data
Silver, Leda.
American origins : tracing our German roots / by Leda Silver.
    p.   cm.
  Includes index.
ISBN 1-56261-150-X : $12.95
1. German Americans—History—Juvenile literature. 2. Immigrants—United States—
History—Juvenile literature. 3 United States—Emigration and immigration—History—
Juvenile literature.
[1. German Americans.] I. Title.
E184.G3S55 1993
973'.0431—dc20
                                 93-30383
                                 CIP
                                 AC

Logo design: Peter Aschwanden
Interior design: Ken Wilson
Illustrations: Beth Evans
Typography: Marcie Pottern
Printer: Guynes Printing Company
Bindery: Prizma Industries, Inc.

Distributed to the book trade by
W. W. Norton & Co., Inc.
500 Fifth Avenue
New York, New York 10110

Distributed to the education market by
The Wright Group
19201 120th Avenue N.E.
Bothell, WA 98011-9512

Cover photo, smiling German refugees, 1938 © The Bettmann Archive
Title page photo, a German American festival in New Jersey, 1940 © The Bettmann Archive
Back cover photo, immigrants arriving in Nebraska © The Bettmann Archive

CONTENTS

THE ADVENTURE BEGINS

America is primarily a nation of immigrants, people who came here from other countries. You can probably think of many of these countries—England, Ireland, Italy, China, and Mexico are a few of them. But do you know which country the most people came from? The answer is Germany. Almost one out of every four Americans has some German ancestry. That means that nearly a quarter of all people in the U.S. had relatives who at one time left Germany to settle in America.

Part I of this book paints a picture of Germany in the old days. Life in the Old World was very orderly. People enjoyed their families. Mealtimes and holidays were important to them. The father was the boss of the family and earned the money, and the mother kept things clean and sparkling and took care of the children. Sons looked to their fathers to see what their own lives would be like. If their fathers were farmers, chances are they would also become farmers. Daughters learned from their mothers how to cook, clean, sew, and make crafts. They grew up to become wives and mothers. It was a very traditional way of life.

The Bettmann Archive

The main street in Lindan, Germany

How Many Germans Came to America?

Decade	Number
1820–1829	5,753
1830–1839	124,726
1840–1849	385,434
1850–1859	976,072
1860–1869	723,734
1870–1879	751,769
1880–1889	1,445,181
1890–1899	579,072
1900–1909	328,722
1910–1919	174,227
1920–1929	386,634
1930–1939	119,107
1940–1949	117,506
1950–1959	576,905
1960–1970	220,248

A total of nearly 7 million Germans immigrated to the U.S. between 1820 and 1970. More people came to America from Germany than from any other country.

The long voyage from Europe to America crossed 4,000 miles of ocean

For hundreds of years, German customs and lifestyles changed little. But beginning in the 1600s, changes in Europe began to threaten the Germans' way of life. Thousands of people started to dream of a better life across the ocean in the New World. Individuals, families, and sometimes even entire villages decided to make the voyage to America.

Some Germans left their homeland in search of religious freedom. Many of the earliest German immigrants settled in the colony begun by William Penn, the founder of Pennsylvania. These people became known as the Pennsylvania Dutch. Other Germans were drawn to America by adventure and the desire to improve their lives. They heard about the new country from family and friends who told them that land was cheap, or even free. Still later immigrants came to America as refugees, fleeing from war and prejudice in their homeland.

Part II tells the story of the German immigrants in the New World. As soon as they arrived, Germans were greeted with many new opportunities—and new challenges. In the beginning, they were shut out by Americans who didn't like them speaking their own language and who were suspicious of their foreign ways. Even Benjamin Franklin, the famous colonial statesman and inventor, complained about the newcomers.

But eventually Germans earned respect and acceptance. They were recognized for being good farmers and expert craftspeople. German immigrants became loyal American citizens. They helped shape nearly all aspects of American life—from religion and holidays to food and music. In fact, German Americans have influenced our culture so much, things that were originally German now just seem American! Let's begin the journey of the German Americans and discover the wealth of contributions they have made to our country.

FAMILY LIFE

Life in Germany hundreds of years ago was very different from life in America today. All over Europe at that time, children were treated as if they were small—even annoying—adults. Their clothes were a smaller version of their parents' clothes. And toys and special books for children were rare.

Most babies and children didn't live long enough to grow up. If a family had ten children, perhaps only two grew to be adults. Others died at birth or as young children from disease or neglect.

For the children who did survive, life was much harder than it is for most American children today. For one thing, most children worked. In fact, the government of Saxony, a German province, tried to force all children to work, but the law was never enacted. Most families put children to work as soon as they could. Young children helped with farm chores, and older kids earned wages to help support

the family. A child as young as four or five could earn a few coins by shooing crows away from the wheat crop or by spinning hemp (a plant) into cord or rope.

Families that were more well-to-do sent their children (usually only their sons) to school. School met six days a week and was very formal. When the teacher entered the classroom, all of the students stood up together and said, "Good morning." If a student wondered about something, he didn't ask. School was not for asking questions, it was for memorizing what the teacher said.

Just as the teacher was in charge of the class, the father was in charge at home. He was the boss of the family, and everyone obeyed his orders. His children were prob-

---

Germans have a long tradition as poets, writers, and storytellers. In fact, many of the fairy tales you probably know are German in origin. Have you ever heard of *Grimm's Fairy Tales*? Jakob and Wilhelm Grimm were the first people to publish "Snow White and the Seven Dwarfs." The two brothers had heard the famous legend for many years before they wrote it down. The story comes from the Hesse region of Germany, where seven hills rise up from the land and are said to be Snow White's hiding place. Between 1812 and 1815, the Brothers Grimm also published "Sleeping Beauty," "Little Red Riding Hood," "Hansel and Gretel," and other favorite tales.

The Bettmann Archive

A boys' school in Berlin

ably a little afraid of him. Women were supposed to care about only three things: *Kirche, Küche, Kinder* (KEER-shuh, KOO-shuh, KIN-duh)—church, kitchen, children.

Families often lived in the same town or village that their great-great-great grandparents had, and sometimes even in the same house! Usually all members of the family—grandparents, aunts, uncles, and cousins—lived in the same town. Families took pride in keeping their homes sparkling clean and their gardens well-tended.

In the Alps and other mountainous regions, people liked to hike. They enjoyed the beautiful scenery and colorful wildflowers. The German people knew that outdoor exercise in natural surroundings was good for *Gesundheit* (ge-ZUHNT-hyt), their health.

Life in the Old Country was predictable and orderly. Boys followed their father's trade or worked the same farm as they became adults. Girls grew up to become

A *village lane in Bavaria*

wives and mothers and make their own homes. For generations, Germans lived a very traditional way of life.

Germans have a long tradition of storytelling

5

GUTEN APPETIT!

Germans often wished each other *"Guten Appetit"* (GOOT-en ah-peh-TEET), which means "Happy eating!" In fact, they had six chances to say it each and every day. Did Germans eat six meals every day? Yes, six mealtimes were possible. But no, no one ate all six meals.

The German diet was very rich. People ladled lots of gravy on their potatoes and dumplings. They liked vegetables covered in a buttery sauce. Many foods were fried. Usually the mother did all the cooking for the family, although her daughters often helped out.

The first meal of the day was *Fruhstuck* (FROO-shtook), breakfast. Families had fresh rolls or bread with butter, cheese, or jam, or sometimes soft-boiled eggs served in a special cup. Eggs cooked any other way, such as scrambled, were for other meals, but not for breakfast. Grown-ups drank coffee or tea with breakfast, and kids had milk.

The Bettmann Archive

A typical German kitchen, around 1850

The mid-morning "second breakfast" was often a slice of bread with butter, topped with another German favorite, a wedge of *Wurst* (vurst), sausage.

The main meal of the day was *Mittagessen* (MEET-ah-GAY-sehn). Unlike the custom in this country to have dinner in the evening, Mittagessen was eaten in the afternoon. The family gathered at the table for a feast, and they took their time about enjoying it, too. School was closed for an hour or two, and so was work.

Germans loved sausage—and they had plenty of choices! Little white sausages made of veal, called *Weissbratwurste* (vees-BRAHT-vurst), had a very delicate flavor. Hardier *Mettwurst* (MAYT-vurst) was spread on bread. Goose liver sausage, *Ganseleberwurst* (gahn-SAYL-eh-bear-vurst), was a special treat. Hundreds of other varieties were fried, poached, or sliced cold.

A family enjoying Mittagessen

Beer halls were popular gathering places

What people ate for Mittagessen depended on what fresh foods were available and also on the regional specialties. In northern Germany, people ate a lot of fish and potatoes, as they did in nearby Scandinavia. In the south, wheat dumplings were a favorite. They were a big hit in neighboring Austria and Switzerland, too. Another favorite German dish was sauerkraut, made of sliced cabbage. Each cook made it a little differently and took pride in her own recipe. Some stewed the cabbage in fruit juice, or even champagne, while others cooked it with oysters.

In the middle of the afternoon, friends often got together for *Kaffee Trinken* (KOF-fay TRINK-en), which actually means "coffee drinking." Sometimes they met at each other's homes, and other times in a café or a pastry shop, called a *Konditorei* (kon-DEE-toh-ree). Pastry cooks and ambitious home bakers concocted rich, fancy desserts, such as cakes with lots of layers and plenty of whipped cream. Black Forest Cherry Cake had so many layers, it was hard to count them all!

The evening meal was simple, usually just bread and butter with cheese, sausage or other meats, and fruit or a salad. Fruit juices for children and adults were popular. The national drink, though, was beer. It was brewed in many light and dark varieties.

The last meal of the day was a little snack before bed, with a nice cup of warm milk or a glass of wine. Good eating was important to Germans, and, unless times were hard, few ever went to bed hungry.

COMMUNITY AND WORK LIFE

Germans felt pride in their home towns and enjoyed a strong sense of belonging. Many towns were fairly small, with populations of 1,000 to 10,000 people. People knew one another and stopped to chat together on the street. Some families had known each other for generations. With such a long history, local customs and traditions grew strong.

Many towns honored a local hero. Augsburg honored Hans Holbein the Elder and Hans Holbein the Younger, father and son artists. Bayreuth's hero was Richard Wagner, the famous composer. In the town of Mainz, they were very proud of Johann Gutenberg. He was a printer who, around 1455, published the first Bible using moveable type. This Bible is thought to be the first book ever printed in Europe. Children learned about these important people in

A milk wagon in Frankfurt

Fierce Doberman pinschers were bred by Germans

People relied on more than just one another in villages and cities. Dogs were cherished as workers and pets. Many popular breeds originated in Germany. Poodles helped hunters retrieve ducks from lakes and ponds, earning them the name *puddler* (POOD-ler). It means "water dog." Dachshunds, with their long, hot-dog-shaped bodies, hunted small animals such as badgers right into their narrow burrows. Huge Great Danes served as guard dogs, and German shepherds and schnauzers were trained to herd sheep and cattle. Ludwig Dobermann bred Doberman pinschers to be fierce-looking guard dogs, and they are still used for protection today.

8

school. Townspeople often named parks or main streets after them and built statues in their honor.

Germans also took pride in their work. They were known for their fine craftsmanship. Guilds, similar to labor unions, ensured that certain crafts and trades were passed from fathers to sons. A young man had to be invited to join the guild before he could follow a trade, such as glassblowing or silversmithing. Only a few men—usually the sons of guild members—were invited to join. The guild members limited membership because they did not want too many craftsmen competing for customers.

German women in small towns and villages almost never worked outside the home at paying jobs. Mothers and daughters did housework, sewed clothes, prepared hearty meals, and took care of the family.

People willing to move to bigger cities found more job opportunities. There, goods such as food, clothing, and furniture were produced in factories. This shift from making things one by one at home to making things in large quantities in factories was called industrialization. It called for new skills and jobs. Some workers helped prepare raw materials, such as wood or cotton, for manufacturing. Still others had jobs that helped transport new goods to marketplaces.

Workers in the cities did not have to join a guild to get these new jobs. If they didn't like a certain job, or they found another boss who paid more, they made a switch. They tried for a better life. When they weren't working, people in cities enjoyed the theater, concerts, and museums.

People in small towns entertained each other. They had a lot of fun at family and community feasts. They enjoyed church societies and musical organizations, such as choirs and instrumental groups. They played games such as skat (a card game) and skittles (a bowling game) at clubs.

The Nuremburg marketplace, around 1900

RELIGION AND HOLIDAYS

Germany sits right in the middle of Europe. For centuries, it was also right in the center of religious conflicts and ideas. In fact, one of the most important religious events in history occurred in Germany in the mid-1500s. It was called the Protestant Reformation. Protestants got their name because they protested the teachings of the Catholic Church.

The Gothardi church in Hildesheim

The Bettmann Archive

But even after the Reformation, Catholics and Protestants argued over their ideas about God. They even went to war. The Thirty Years War (1618–1648) was fought all over Europe, but the worst battles were in Germany because it was in the middle of things. The war caused terrible destruction. By the time it was over, German cities and towns lay in ruins. Crops and trade routes had been devastated. More than 5 million people had been killed.

Most Protestants lived in the northern part of Germany, and most Catholics lived in the south. Besides their religious differences, the north and south had different personalities. People in the north thought of themselves as polite, modern, and ambitious. In the south, Germans described themselves as friendly, warm-hearted, and jovial.

But not everyone in Germany was Christian. Jewish communities could be found throughout the country, most in cities along the Rhine River. Sometimes Jews were forced to live in segregated ghettoes by leaders who were anti-Semitic,

---

Martin Luther (1483–1546) posted a notice on the door of the castle church in Wittenberg in 1517. He wanted to debate 95 points about the Catholic Church he disagreed with. He ignited a religious revolution called the Protestant Reformation that spread throughout Western Europe in the 1500s. It led to greater freedom of religious dissent, which meant people felt freer to say what they believed about God and the Church. Luther founded the Lutheran Church, and he translated the Bible from Latin into German, the language of everyday people.

which means they hated Jews simply because they were Jewish.

Holidays were joyfully celebrated in Germany. St. Nicholas, the patron saint of children, was honored with a feast day on December 6. German children put one of their shoes on the fireplace or a windowsill before they went to sleep. They hoped to find it filled with treats from St. Nicholas on the next morning. Does this custom sound familiar? St. Nicholas became Santa Claus in America. Germans also loved to decorate the *tannenbaum* (TAHN-en-baum), the Christmas tree, a favorite holiday custom they brought with them to the New World.

In late November many families celebrated Advent. They put four candles on a traditional wreath and decorated it with bright red ribbons. Then they attached it to a chandelier in the living room or set it on a table. Each Sunday before Christmas the family got together and lit one candle for the week.

Decorating the Christmas tree

Catholic areas of Germany enjoyed Karneval, which was similar to a carnival or a Mardi Gras celebration. It was a time of fun and feasts before Lent. The Prince and Princess of the parade led fancy floats, musical bands, and jesters wearing funny masks. It took a lot of work to plan all this festivity. The organizers met for the first time at 11 minutes after 11 p.m. on the 11th day of the 11th month (November). They worked hard until spring, when at last they began the merriment.

Martin Luther posting his notice on the church door

THE GERMAN NATION

We think of Germany as a nation now, but until 1871 it was a hodgepodge of cities and states that ruled themselves. Centuries ago, people's identity came from their village, city, or region. People thought of themselves as Bavarians or Württembergers or Saxons, not Germans. Often, different regions were rivals and sometimes went to war with each other. Bavarians and Prussians, for example, had a long history of conflict.

In those times, German cities were often attacked by thieves, criminals, and rival political groups that wanted power. To protect themselves, many cities built walls and gates. The town of Lubeck, for example, built the famous Holsten Gate in 1477. Trier, one of Germany's oldest cities, was founded around 2500 B.C. Its location at the meeting point of three rivers—the Mosel, Saar, and Ruwar—made it very desirable. Imagine how many enemies lurked about and tried to conquer it over all those years.

Sometimes a city's enemy lived only 20 or 30 miles away. That doesn't seem very far to us now, but hundreds of years ago, when people traveled by foot or on horseback, it was considered a great distance.

During the 1700s, how many different governments do you think were running Germany? One? Two? Ten? The answer is more than 300! The country was like a huge patchwork quilt. Each area was unique and ruled by a different leader.

Sometimes these city-states banded together for trade. Hamburg, a great city near the mouth of the Elbe River, joined the Hanseatic League. This association helped the merchants and craftsmen in Hamburg sell their goods to nearby cities. It also helped them buy what the other members of the Hanseatic League had for sale.

The old city wall in Trier

The Bettmann Archive

More than High German united the patchwork quilt of Germany. Germans shared elements of culture and heritage, too. Every German child grew up learning the fantastic legend of the great hero Siegfried. At an old castle high on a mountain near the Rhine River, Siegfried slew a terrible dragon. Then he bathed in the dragon's blood. This gave him superhuman strength and the magical power to understand birds and other animals in the forest.

But whether they were from Hamburg or Trier or Lubeck, Germans did have one thing in common: the German language. In fact, there were two German languages, one called *Hochdeutsch* (HOHK-doych), which means "High German," and one known as *Platt Deutsch* (PLAHT doych), or "Low German."

In each region, people spoke a different dialect of Low German with their family and friends. These dialects were very different from one another. If someone from Pforzheim visited another city, such as Munster, the language sounded quite foreign and impossible to understand. That's where High German came in.

If visitors wanted to make themselves understood in a different region, they spoke High German. It was the correct, well-educated way of speaking that people used at work and in formal situations. It was quite different from the regional Low German they spoke informally. High German was the strongest common bond among all the German-speaking states. But even though they shared a common language, people could tell what region someone was from as soon as he or she spoke. Their accents gave them away!

A street in Frankfurt

The legendary hero Siegfried slaying a dragon

THE THREE B's OF MUSIC

Johann Sebastian Bach (1685–1750)
Does your family have a family business? For the Bachs it was music. They carried their musical tradition on for seven generations. That's more than 200 years! Johann Sebastian Bach was the most gifted of them all.

J. S. Bach was born on March 21, 1685, in Eisenach. His father and mother died when he was only ten, and he went to live with his older brother, Johann Christoph, who played the organ. Johann Sebastian studied composition and learned to play the organ, violin, and clavier (a stringed keyboard instrument). He attended all the concerts he could, sometimes walking many, many miles to get there.

In 1708 Bach got an important job at the chapel of the duke in Weimar. He held this position for nine years and composed some of the greatest organ music of all time. He became a virtuoso, which means a master musician, and toured Germany.

Bach moved to the city of Cothen, and then later to Leipzig. He had a hard life and a difficult time supporting his large family. After his first wife died, he married again and in all had 20 children, although not all of them lived to adulthood. Yet despite his day-to-day troubles, he composed the world-famous *Brandenburg Concertos* and other great works for organ and chamber orchestras. When he died in Leipzig in 1750, he left behind a wealth of music that moves people as much today as it did the first day it was performed.

Johann Sebastian Bach

Ludwig von Beethoven (1770–1827)
Born in Bonn on December 16, 1770, Beethoven made his way to Vienna, the great center of music and culture, when he was 22 years old. He felt awkward and was self-conscious about his appearance. He looked older than he was and had bad manners. Yet he became a virtuoso piano player and was welcomed at palaces by nobility.

Although he never married, Beethoven was in love with different women and wrote musical tributes to them. To one he dedicated "Moonlight Sonata." "Für Elise," written for the daughter of a friend, means "For Elizabeth." When he died in Vienna on

March 26, 1827, a passionate love letter he had written was discovered. To whom was he writing? It is still a mystery.

The tragic irony of Beethoven's life was that he began to lose his hearing when he was about 30 years old. By the time he was 50, he was completely deaf. Forced to give up playing the piano, he expressed his creativity by composing some of the greatest music ever written. He is most famous for his nine symphonies, among them the dramatic Eroica, the Fifth, and the Ninth.

Johannes Brahms (1833–1897)

Johannes Brahms was born in Hamburg on May 7, 1833. When he was just six years old, he invented his own musical notation. He wanted to write down the melodies that he composed in his head. Soon, young Brahms helped support his struggling family by playing piano late at night in taverns and inns.

Ludwig von Beethoven

Johannes Brahms

At 20 he met the distinguished musicians Robert and Clara Schumann in Düsseldorf. They thought he was a genius, helped his career, and treated him as a son. In return, Brahms was a devoted friend. When Robert became ill and died, Brahms rushed to help. He took an apartment above the Schumanns' place and helped Clara and the children.

Brahms was strongly influenced by Beethoven. People loved his emotional symphonies and continue to listen to them a century later. One of his masterpieces was *German Requiem*. Some of Brahms' most wonderful compositions—the lullabies and waltzes—were created for his friends' children.

THE QUEST FOR FREEDOM

During the 1600s and early 1700s, life became very difficult for people in southwestern Germany. Overpopulation in the wine-growing regions made it hard to make a living, because more and more people were competing for the same jobs. Government taxes were very high, burdening families who already struggled to make ends meet. A costly war with France's King Louis XIV had taken many lives and destroyed towns. And the winter of 1708–1709 was brutal.

People were growing desperate. They learned that other Europeans were migrating to the New World, where freedom and the chance to make a living awaited them. They decided to leave behind what was familiar and begin their lives anew.

By 1709, about 13,000 people from the Palatinate area in western Germany had traveled down the Rhine River, headed for a port to begin the voyage to the New World.

Many crossed the North Sea to England, where they boarded ships bound for America. They often traveled in family groups, and sometimes whole villages went together. The trip down the Rhine took four to six weeks. In many cases it took all their money.

Other Germans left their homeland for religious reasons. During the late 1700s, thousands of Germans began searching for a place where they could practice their religion openly, free from hostility or persecution. William Penn promised them such a place in his Quaker colony. Penn traveled from Pennsylvania, which he helped found in 1681, to the Rhine Valley in Germany. There, he preached to dissenters from the established Protestant churches and encouraged them to join his colony. Many of these people were weary of moving from country to country in Europe, searching for greater religious freedom. They decided to follow William Penn to the New World.

Some poor Germans had to beg for food

The colonial emigrant Gottlieb Mittelberger kept a detailed journal of his experiences journeying from Germany to America in 1750. He recorded first-hand the many difficulties that faced these early travelers. For example, when people died during the voyage, their spouses had to work off their redemptioner contracts. If a father and mother both perished, their orphaned children had to repay their parents' debt by working for many years.

Leaving for the New Country

But getting to America was not as easy as deciding to go. Many farmers, laborers, and other people did not have enough money for the transatlantic trip. They were convinced to make the journey by agents called "new landers," who were paid by the shippers to fill their ships with human "cargoes." The new landers told the poor travelers that they could pay for their fare by becoming "redemptioners."

Redemptioners had two choices. They could pay for the trip within two weeks after they arrived in the New World. This option helped people who had relatives in America who could lend or give them the money.

But not everyone was so lucky. The other option for redemptioners was much more common. They could have their fare paid by an American colonist. In return, they would have to work for that colonist for a certain amount of time. It was not unusual for redemptioners to work for four years or more to repay their debt.

More than one-half of the Germans who immigrated to America in colonial times worked as redemptioners to get there. In fact, over time, Germans themselves became the purchasers of new redemptioners from Germany.

Gottlieb Mittelberger kept a journal of his voyage

REVOLUTION!

The next great surge of German immigration happened in the mid-1800s. All over Europe, people were staging uprisings against their leaders. They wanted to govern themselves.

Germany was a part of this upheaval. It all started in 1815, when many German-speaking states met together in a large assembly called the Congress of Vienna. There, they formed the German Confederation. It was supposed to take the place of the Holy Roman Empire, which had dominated Germany for centuries.

But the Confederation had trouble—big trouble. Many small German states wanted to rule themselves. They led a national movement to create a unified Germany in which all states would have a say. But the two major European powers of the time, Prussia and Austria, wanted to control them. The leader of Austria stomped out the movement to keep his power.

People were very angry. During the years 1848 and 1849, they led a revolution. But Prussia fought hard against them. The rebels couldn't rouse enough support from fellow Germans, and their revolution failed. In 1851, the government returned to its previous form, the German Confederation.

Revolutionary leaders who had written or spoken out in favor of the new ideas and against the Confederation were in danger from those in power. These rebels were called "forty-eighters," after the year the revolution started. They were from southwestern Germany and the Rhineland. The forty-eighters had to flee for their lives.

During the 1848 Revolution, there were many brave Kreigers (KREE-gers), which means "warriors." Kreiger is also a last name. Many Germans originally named themselves after the occupation of the father of the family. Perhaps you know someone who has one of the last names listed below—or maybe your own family name is on this list. (The first pronunciation given is German. The second, if it's different, is English.)

Bader (BAH-der, BAY-der), barber
Brenner (BREHN-ner), distiller
Richter (REECK-ter, RICK-ter), judge
Roth (roht, roth), red
Saltz (sahlts), salt maker
Sandler (SAHND-ler, SAND-ler), cobbler
Schneider (SHNY-der), tailor
Stein (shteen, stine or steen), stone
Weber (VAY-ber, WEB-er), weaver

Brave Kreigers of the 1848 Revolution

Revolutionary soldiers fought the king's army in 1848

Many Germans decided to leave their home in those troubling times of war to try their luck in America. They were sick of paying high taxes to fund the armies. Their farms and homelands had been ravaged by fighting. They had seen too many people die because of soldiers, disease, and famine. A few even left to escape being drafted into the army.

For other reasons as well, Germans began to head for America in record numbers. In the 1840s, the so-called "Old Lutherans" left Saxony, a German province, mainly for religious reasons. At about the same time, Jews—about 10,000 from Bavaria alone—left to seek better jobs and living conditions, and freedom from anti-Semitism.

Of the many Germans who decided to go to America, the forty-eighters were to have the biggest impact. Many had university educations. Some, such as the leader Carl Schurz, were skilled at writing about politics in the newspapers. They were radical and revolutionary, used to stirring up people's feelings in order to create change. In Germany they had tried for national unity but failed. In America they would fight against slavery and succeed.

Rebels often made speeches in beer halls

19

THE LATE 1800s

An emigrant is someone who leaves the country he or she is *from*. An immigrant is someone who moves *to* a new country. After the 1848 Revolution, hundreds of thousands of Germans emigrated from Germany for a chance in America. What was going on in Germany that made so many people decide to leave?

People wanted more political freedom. They were tired of being ruled by monarchs and aristocrats, leaders who had titles such as "Lord" and "Duke." Like many other people in Europe at the time, Germans wanted to rule themselves. They wanted democracy. Sometimes citizens even staged uprisings to try to gain power. But when their efforts to improve their lives failed time after time, many decided to leave Germany.

Farmers began to emigrate in great numbers, too. Though they loved their villages and their simple country lives, they could no longer support their families. Farms were getting smaller and smaller, because laws about inheritance had changed. For centuries, one person, usually the oldest son, inherited the farm when the owner died. In this way, farms were passed down through many generations. But new rules required that the land be divided among all the survivors, called heirs. So, for example, if a farmer had six children, each heir would receive one-sixth of the farm. If each of those children had six children, the land was further divided into even smaller plots. After a few generations, there was no more land to divide.

But there was a place where land was abundant. German farmers heard from relatives and friends in America who told them that land was plentiful and cheap

Gathering hay on a German farm

The Bettmann Archive

In the 1800s, American businessmen published guidebooks and newspapers in German to attract Germans to come to America. They wanted cheap labor and people to settle in their growing railroad towns. These guidebooks and newspapers offered travel advice and information—not all of it true—about the new land. They reprinted letters written by people who had already made the move to America. As more Germans were able to read about the faraway land, more made the decision to pack up and go.

there. Many Germans started to dream of a better life in the New World.

It also became easier to emigrate than it had been before. During the mid-1800s, strict laws about leaving Germany were lfted, and transportation improved. Sailing ships were no longer the only way to get to America. Steamships started to cross the Atlantic Ocean as well. They were faster, cheaper, and made the trip much more comfortable.

Most Germans who left for America before the mid-1800s were farmers, peasants, and laborers from southwest Germany. But after about 1850, the majority who left were city folks from all over Germany. They had experience working in shops and factories, and many were educated. The people who made up the largest wave of German immigration were a much more diverse group than the early immigrants had been.

In all, more than 5 million Germans immigrated to the United States in the 1800s. By 1900, one out of every four immigrants in the United States was from Germany. Those who stayed in the Old Country had busy lives. But they still

The Bettmann Archive

Harvesting hops

thought of their friends and relatives thousands of miles away, making new lives in a new land.

Guidebooks about the U.S. drew many Germans to American shores

VOYAGE TO A NEW LAND

Before steamships were invented in the mid-1800s, the voyage from Europe to America took from one to three months. Sailing ships were cramped and dirty. In fact, they were built to carry cargo, not people. These ships transported raw materials from America to Europe, then carried manufactured goods back to America. But goods took up much less room than raw materials. So shippers packed their extra cargo space with human beings—European emigrants eager to reach America.

Some passengers were wary about making the long voyage in the dark cargo hulls below deck, called steerage. But shippers lured them with promises that food, money, or land would be free for the taking once they got to America. Some people believed these lies. Others had no choice but to make the journey. They had spent a lot of money just getting to a port city, or had paid heavy fees to get legal papers to leave. Some people were robbed while

Immigrants waiting at Ellis Island

Not all immigrants stayed in the U.S.

Not all Germans who arrived in America stayed here. About one in eight returned to Europe. After such a grueling voyage, why would they go back? For some, life in America was harder than they expected. If they'd heard that "the streets were paved with gold"—a common myth about the New World—they were in for a bitter disappointment. Many immigrants had a hard time finding a decent job. The language and the customs were strange to them. So, homesick and bewildered, they crossed the ocean again to return to what they knew.

traveling, so they were penniless when they reached the ship. Others were leaving Germany illegally and feared being caught if they tried to return home. For all of these reasons, most people were determined to make the great voyage, no matter the cost.

And the cost was immense. In cash, it took all that many people had. Others signed up to be redemptioners. They promised to repay the cost of the journey by working once they got to America.

But the journey took its toll in more than money. In steerage, there was little water for bathing and too few chamber pots (portable toilets). The smells were intense and awful in the airless quarters. Often, the immigrants didn't have enough food or water. The ships rode the waves up and down, and lurched and rocked during storms. People got terribly seasick.

Diseases spread quickly in these crowded quarters. Cholera and smallpox raged. So many Germans died of typhus, it became known as "Palatine fever," after the Palatinate region of Germany. Passengers crammed together to sleep in spaces just six feet by two feet. Lice were so thick they had to be scraped off people's bodies. Many people died during the voyage. Because there was no place to bury the bodies, they were thrown overboard into the sea.

The journey was especially brutal for children. In his journal, the emigrant Gottlieb Mittleberger wrote that 32 young children died on his ship. He concluded that it was almost impossible for children from one to seven years old to survive the voyage.

Ellis Island, N.Y.

But the strong and lucky ones reached American shores. Many immigrants' first glimpse of their new country was either New York City or Ellis Island in New York Harbor. For others, it was New Orleans, Louisiana. From this southern city they rode empty Mississippi riverboats up to northern cargo points. Their long, difficult journey was finally over. But their challenges had just begun.

Conditions were harsh on immigrant ships

23

PENNSYLVANIA DUTCH

Among the first German immigrants to reach America were the so-called "Pennsylvania Dutch." Dutch? Yes, the mix-up came from the word *Deutsche* (doych), which means "German" in that language. "Dutch" is an American mispronunciation, but the name stuck. In fact, many ethnic Germans were nicknamed "Dutch."

In the late 1600s, about 100,000 German settlers arrived in southeast Pennsylvania. America was still in its colonial period. These early German settlers were religious dissenters who disagreed with the established Protestant churches. They were drawn to Pennsylvania because it was a haven for people seeking religious freedom. They wanted to practice their own religious beliefs within their own communities.

In many ways the Pennsylvania Dutch were different from other German immi-

Over time, the influence of the Pennsylvania Dutch touched the rest of the country. Do you like German chocolate cake? That food, as well as coleslaw, originated with the Pennyslvania Dutch. Their artisans became well-known for their glassware, furniture, clocks, pottery, and pewterware. Furniture, wooden boxes, and barns were often decorated with colorful designs called "hex signs." These designs came from Europe, where they were used during the Middle Ages (the 400s through the 1400s) to ward off evil spirits. The Pennsylvania Dutch, however, simply used them to add cheer to their plain surroundings. Hex signs often feature stars and other geometric figures, and bold, primary colors.

The Bettmann Archive

Driving through Pennsylvania farm country

grants. Most Germans did not come to America because of religious persecution, although many German Jews fled Europe to escape anti-Semitism. Most Germans who came to the U.S. were either Catholic or belonged to the two main German Protestant churches, the Lutheran and the Reformed.

The Pennsylvania Dutch were different from other German immigrants in two other ways as well. They were pacifists, which meant they were against wars of any kind. They also distrusted government and disliked outside rules and regulations. They wanted to live their own lives apart from mainstream settlements.

The Amish are one such group of Pennsylvania Dutch who wanted to live undisturbed in their own communities. They have lived apart from the rest of American society since colonial times. Even today, their lives in farm communities are much like the lives of the early settlers. They wear old-fashioned plain black clothes, and they drive black horse-drawn carriages, never cars. They do not listen to modern music, go to movies, or own televisions. Amish children are educated at home, where they are taught to preserve their way of life. They are very religious.

Mennonite women walking to church

The Mennonites, like the Amish, live in their own communities, too. In 1683, a handful of Mennonite and Quaker families founded Germantown, Pennsylvania, which is now part of Philadelphia. Swiss Mennonites got a grant of 10,000 acres in Lancaster County. Less well-known groups also sought religious freedom in the colony. In 1719 an Anabaptist group called Westphalian Dunkards migrated here. Schwenkfelders came in 1734. And the Moravians—more than 700 strong— founded two cities in Pennsylvania, Bethlehem and Nazareth.

The Pennsylvania Dutch were excellent farmers and made almost everything they needed. Each member of the family had a part to play. Women took care of the children, spun their own cloth, made clothes for the family, dried and preserved fruits, cooked all the meals, and tended vegetable gardens and orchards.

A typical Pennsylvania Dutch barn

COLONIAL IMMIGRANTS

The Pennsylvania Dutch were not the only early immigrants to come to America. Thousands of other German immigrants came to the New World when America was still a British colony, before the Revolutionary War (1775–1783). In fact, many German Americans fought for American independence.

One of the most famous of these was a woman, Maria Ludwig. She traveled with her husband, a gunner in the army, and carried pitchers of water to grateful soldiers in battle. That's how she earned her nickname, "Molly Pitcher." She took her husband's place at the cannon after he was wounded in battle. Even George Washington later noted her bravery.

Other Germans fought against American independence. The British paid about

"Molly Pitcher," Revolutionary War heroine

30,000 Hessian soldiers from Germany to fight on their side. But even though they had fought for the British, after the war about 5,000 of them decided to stay in America. They settled in areas where other German immigrants lived and fit right in.

Angry colonists burned Zenger's newspaper

John Peter Zenger, who immigrated to America at age 13, published a little newspaper called the *New York Weekly Journal*. In it, he criticized the dishonest governor—and got into big trouble. He was put in jail in 1733. His lawyer argued that the Zenger trial was really about the right to free speech itself, not just the freedom of one journalist. (Free speech is the right to say what you believe without fearing the government will hurt or jail you.) They won the case, setting an important foundation for free speech in America.

Not everyone was pleased with the number of Germans immigrating to America. In fact, the powerful statesman Benjamin Franklin was furious because the German immigrants usually voted the same—and not always for him! Franklin tried to get others to share his strong anti-German feelings. In 1751, he wrote a pamphlet in which he called the Germans "boors" (a boor is a crude, stupid person) and predicted that they would "Germanize" Americans rather than adopt American ways.

This anti-German sentiment was tough for the new immigrants to take. But not everything was bleak. They were a minority, but a fairly large one, so they had power. By the mid-1700s, about one-third of the population of Pennsylvania was German. In addition, in some ways they were respected. They had a reputation for hard work, thrift, and fine craftsmanship. German immigrants were very adept at certain trades, such as glassmaking. The first paper mill was set up by a German. And the first Bible published in America was printed by a German, in the German language.

The famous Conestoga wagon was built by Germans, too. Named after Conestoga Creek, Pennsylvania, the wagon was built to haul farm produce. It was large and rugged, covered by canvas draped over high arching hoops. It took six strong horses to pull its 3,000-pound frame. During the 1700s, sometimes a hundred or more wagons a day would file into Philadelphia loaded with fruits and vegetables for sale. Conestogas became famous later as the covered wagons that transported American pioneers west to the frontier.

German Americans were also recognized as skilled farmers. Their farm animals were not allowed to roam freely, which was the custom, but kept in huge barns. One man wrote at the time that the farms of Germans had bigger orchards and more fertile fields than other people's, and had "a general appearance of plenty and neatness in everything. . . ."

The Bettmann Archive

Germans built the first Conestoga wagons

BEGINNING A NEW LIFE

The largest wave of German immigrants arrived in America between 1850 and 1900. For these "greenhorns," as new immigrants were called, America was a strange and sometimes unfriendly place. They had to find a job and a place to live. They had to learn new rules and a foreign language. But before they could meet any of these challenges, they had to be legally admitted to the United States. For millions of immigrants, this took place at Castle Garden and Ellis Island, both in New York Harbor.

These enormous centers processed up to 5,000 immigrants a day. Unfortunately, a huge fire at Ellis Island in 1897 destroyed all the immigration records. Many families' documents were lost forever.

Weary and sometimes even sick after their long voyage, the newcomers first had to pass a medical examination. If the health officer discovered that they were

Jubilant immigrants wave U.S. flags

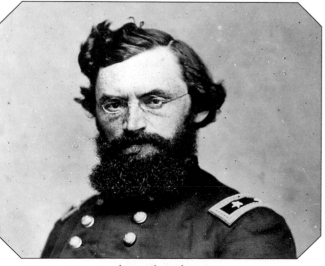

Major General Carl Schurz

Carl Schurz arrived in America in 1852 and became one of the most important citizens in his adopted land. The famous forty-eighter helped Abraham Lincoln get elected President. Schurz was a general in the Union Army during the Civil War, was elected a senator of Missouri, and was appointed Secretary of the Interior. He edited a German-language newspaper in St. Louis and then edited the *New York Evening Post* and *Harper's Weekly*.

28

seriously ill, they would be labeled "undesirable." Next, they waited in another long line to be questioned by an immigration official. What were their skills? Did they have family in America? Where did they plan to settle? The officials usually spoke to the immigrants in English, a language they did not understand. If the officials discovered that they had broken the law, they would again be labeled "undesirable." The U.S. government didn't want to support people who were criminals, or who could not work or take care of themselves. The "undesirables" were forced to return to Europe.

But most immigrants passed the grueling inspections and left the processing centers as legal residents of the U.S. Next, they had to decide where to settle. If they had family or friends here, they usually traveled to join them. If they wanted land for farming, they set out for the Midwest. Because New York City offered an exciting culture and many jobs in industry, many Germans settled there and never left. Spillover communities grew in nearby Hoboken, Newark, and Jersey City, New Jersey. The

growing cities of Pittsburgh, Louisville, and Cincinnati attracted many Germans as well. So many Germans settled in the area between New York City, Minneapolis, St. Louis, and Baltimore that it was called the "German Quadrangle."

German immigrants who settled in the cities tended to live near other Germans. They kept many of their Old Country ways alive. They spoke German and read German newspapers. They lived in areas called "Over the Rhine" or "Little Germany." They found comfort in living apart from other immigrant groups or American-born citizens. Just as the Americans seemed foreign to the Germans, the new immigrants seemed foreign to the Americans. They eyed the newcomers suspiciously and made them feel unwelcome.

The new language and customs of their adopted land took a lot of time to learn. Sometimes the parents of an immigrant family—the first generation—never fully adopted American ways or learned to speak English. Often it was the children—the second generation—who adapted most easily.

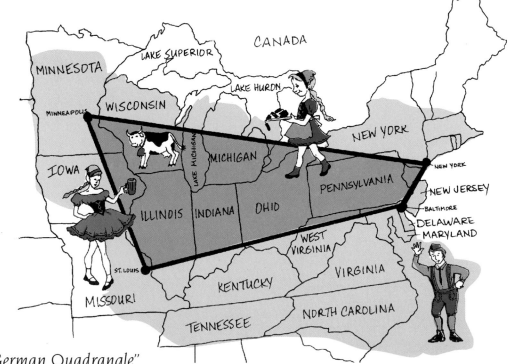

The so-called "German Quadrangle"

SETTLING THE MIDWEST

Besides Pennsylvania, the other main area of German settlement was the Midwest—Ohio, Indiana, Illinois, Michigan, Nebraska, Iowa, Minnesota, and Wisconsin. Wisconsin was a special favorite because land was cheap there.

New settlers in Nebraska

German farmers by the thousands settled on the Great Plains. In fact, by 1900 most of the farmers in America were of German ancestry. The new immigrants often joined small communities of fellow Germans, and descendants of Germans, on the prairies. It made them feel more comfortable in the new land to share language and cultural ties with their neighbors.

The pioneers on the prairies faced a number of challenges and hardships. If they were homesteaders, they had 160 acres on the wide, lonely prairie and few neighbors. The weather in the Midwest was extreme, threatening crops and sometimes even lives. Blinding blizzards in the winter added to people's isolation, and drought during the summer made them worry about their livestock. Prairie fires could strike day or night. Money was tight, and they had to struggle to pay for the things they couldn't make, such as farm equipment, coffee beans, and certain fabrics. Although it was tough on the Plains, German settlers were determined not to give up.

Stagecoaches were one common way of crossing the wide open prairies of the Western frontier. But travelers had to follow some rules. In 1877 the *Omaha Herald* newspaper offered this advice to stagecoach passengers:

"The best seat in a stage is the one next to the driver. If the team runs away—sit still and take your chances. If you jump, nine out of ten times you will get hurt. Don't smoke a strong pipe inside the coach—spit on the leeward side. Don't lop over neighbors when sleeping. Never shoot on the road as the noise might frighten the horses. Don't discuss politics or religion. Don't grease your hair, because travel is dusty."

Wisconsin farmland attracted many German immigrants

One thing that helped them during tough times was the old country tradition of everyone pitching in. Women and children did farm work along with men. The hard labor paid off. Their farms prospered. They were on their way to success in America.

After the Civil War (1861–1865), new immigrants were still drawn to the Midwest, but not because of farming. New farm land had become scarce—most of it had been taken by homesteaders and settlers. New German immigrants poured into Midwestern cities and towns because there were thriving German communities. In 1850, three out of every ten people in Milwaukee and St. Louis had been born in Germany.

Texas drew a lot of Germans as well. In 1831 a settler near Houston sent a letter to his friend in the Old Country. The enthusiastic description was published in a newspaper and later in a book. It attracted many new settlers. Fifty years later, in the 1880s, what had been plantation land was divided up and sold. The new railroad allowed more people to settle in the area, too. Immigrants from many countries came to take advantage of these opportunities.

Life in Texas was sometimes hard. A note was found on a deserted cabin in 1886. It said, "350 miles to the nearest post office—100 miles to wood—20 miles to water—6 inches to hell. God bless our home! Gone to live with wife's folks."

A *bumpy ride*

31

PREJUDICE DURING WORLD WAR I

By the early twentieth century, German communities in America were doing well. But World War I (1914–1918) brought a big change. America and its allies went to war against Germany and its allies. People in the U.S. were very angry about their enemies across the ocean and distrusted anything German.

Americans even became suspicious of U.S. citizens of German ancestry, especially those who had worked to keep German traditions alive. Mobs threatened and ridiculed German Americans. They called them "Huns," after Atilla the Hun, the bloodthirsty German warrior king who ruled in the fifth century.

During the war, pressure was put on anyone and anything that was German. For example, frankfurters (sausages that had come from Frankfurt, Germany) were renamed. They became all-American hot dogs. Even hamburgers, because their name came from Hamburg, a large city in Germany, were called "liberty burgers" or "Salisbury steaks."

German-American newspapers lost advertisers and readers, and began to go out of business. German books were removed from the shelves of libraries. German language courses in public schools were canceled. Some states even outlawed speaking the language in public. Wedding marches by Mendelssohn and Wagner, famous German composers, were no longer used in marriage ceremonies. Some German Americans were tarred and feath-

The Bettmann Archive

Taking the oath of citizenship

ered in their communities, and their homes were ransacked.

President Woodrow Wilson also spoke out against "hyphenated Americans." (He was referring to the fact that "German-

---

During the wave of anti-German prejudice during WWI, many German families changed their last names to make them sound more "American." Here are a few of the common German names that became Americanized:

Schmitt became Smith
Roth—Ross
Wasser—Waters
Stein—Stone
Konig—King
Jong—Young
Heinrich—Henry
Brunn—Brown

American" was spelled with a hyphen.) Theodore Roosevelt was suspicious of German Americans, too. He said, "The men of German blood who have tried to be both Germans and Americans are no Americans at all, but traitors to America and tools and servants of Germany against America."

Most German Americans reacted to this hostility by giving up their cultural ties with Germany and their German traditions. They tried hard to become full-fledged Americans. They proclaimed their loyalty to the U.S. Some people, and even some companies, changed their names. "German-American" banks began to call themselves "North American" banks. In New York, the "Germania Life Insurance Company" became the "Guardian Life Insurance Company."

Trench soldiers in World War I

Other German Americans didn't want to take sides against their old homeland or give up their German customs. They organized the German-American Central Alliance. Its main purpose was not to support Germany, but to fight Prohibition.

Prohibition was a law that banned all alcohol—including beer, the favorite German drink. The German-American Central Alliance saw Prohibition as another example of anti-German prejudice, and a threat to their way of life. They fought against Prohibition, but lost. From 1919 to 1933, it was illegal to make, sell, or drink alcohol in the U.S.

When the U.S. entered the war in 1917, German Americans showed they were patriotic. Thousands of them enlisted in the army. They fought valiantly against Germany and its allies, and many died. One famous leader of the American Army was General John J. Pershing. A German American himself, his family name had once been Pfoerschin.

During World War I, German Americans faced prejudice

WORLD WAR II REFUGEES

When Adolf Hitler and the Nazis came to power in 1933, a new wave of immigrants began to flee Germany. The Nazis took complete control of German society, jailed anyone who disagreed with them, and spread hatred of Jews. Hitler set up concentration camps throughout Germany, where he ordered the deaths of 6 million Jews and thousands of other people the Nazis labeled "undesirable." Some of the world's leading scientists, artists, and scholars fled for their lives.

Most of the German refugees who came to America during this time were Jewish. The scientist Albert Einstein is the most famous. Maurice Goldhaber, also a physicist, came too. After the danger in his native country, he was amazed by the freedom and opportunity in America. He could even buy a vacuum tube for his nuclear research at the corner drugstore!

Physicists from all over Europe immigrated to America to escape Hitler as his army invaded country after country during World War II (1939–1945). One group of scientists worked together at Los Alamos, New Mexico, in secret war-time efforts to beat the Nazis to nuclear power. They succeeded, becoming the first to produce an atomic bomb. President Harry Truman ordered this bomb to be dropped on Germany's war-time partner, Japan, to end the war. With this act, a new and very dangerous era for the whole world began.

Other German refugees were experts in the new field of psychology, the study of how human beings behave and feel. During the 1930s, about 250 of these scholars and doctors came to America from Germany and Austria. Some of them treated people

Hitler addressing a rally in 1938

The psychologist Bruno Bettelheim was another World War II refugee from Germany. He arrived in 1939 after spending a year in a Nazi concentration camp. Based on his experiences there, he wrote about how people can be persuaded to do horrible things they would not normally do on their own. General Dwight D. Eisenhower was a descendant of German immigrants himself who later was elected president. He considered Bettelheim's report so important, he ordered all U.S. military officials stationed in Europe to read it.

German author Thomas Mann

with emotional problems. They encouraged their patients to delve into their dreams and childhood memories to get to the root of their problems. This method is called psychoanalysis and is still widely used today.

Many non-Jewish Germans also sought refuge. Thomas Mann, the author of *The Magic Mountain* and a Nobel Prize winner, spent years in Los Angeles. He said he saw more German writers there than he had ever seen in Munich. His neighbors were famous exiles as well: the composer Arnold Schönberg, the writer Franz Werfel, the conductor Bruno Walter, and the playwright Berthold Brecht. Paul Tillich, a religious writer, was another intellectual who crossed the ocean and brought his ideas.

Like the German immigrants who came here after the failed revolution in 1848, the refugees in the 1930s were committed to democracy. They sadly gave up their ties to Germany because they hated the Nazis and what they stood for.

When World War II broke out, there was some anti-German feeling in the United States, but it was nothing at all like the craziness and prejudice during World War I. By the 1940s, German Americans were assimilated, which means they had blended into American society. Other Americans did not suspect them of being disloyal as they had a generation before.

Many World War II refugees were psychologists and psychoanalysts

MILWAUKEE, WISCONSIN

No city in the U.S. shows the influence of German Americans more than Milwaukee, Wisconsin. Cheerful taverns can be found on nearly every busy street. People gather there to dance the polka, chat with old friends, and enjoy concerts featuring the zither, a stringed instrument that came from Germany.

Grocery stores carry all kinds of brat—that's short for bratwurst, a spicy German sausage. It's served in a bun like a hot dog and often smothered with grilled onions or sauerkraut. People buy them in the stands at Milwaukee's County Stadium as they watch the Milwaukee Brewers play baseball.

During Oktoberfest, an autumn celebration, people dress up in dirndls and lederhosen, traditional German skirts and leather shorts. They dance to favorite German tunes and drink fancy German beers.

Taverns, sausage, beer—it all sounds pretty German, doesn't it? Milwaukee is a true German American city. Over the years, huge numbers of German immigrants settled in Milwaukee and southeastern Wisconsin. In fact, by the 1880s more Milwaukeans read a German-language newspaper than one in English.

Milwaukee is a major Great Lakes port. The city takes its name from "*Mahn-a-waukee Seepe*," a Native American phrase that means "gathering place by the river." One of the main industries in Milwaukee is—you guessed it—brewing beer. In the 1840s Jacob Best and his sons immigrated to the city. After they got settled, they introduced lager beer. It was an instant hit and has been popular ever since. In addition to the

German influence was very strong in Milwaukee and the rest of Wisconsin, but these weren't the only places where German immigrants made their mark. Guess which states have a city called Germantown:

1. Kentucky
2. Illinois
3. Maryland
4. New York
5. Pennsylvania
6. Tennessee
7. Wisconsin

Answer: All of them!

The Bettmann Archive

Many Germans settled in Milwaukee

Best brewery, Miller, Schlitz, Blatz, and Pabst are all located in Milwaukee.

Milwaukee came to be known as the "beer capital" of the United States in the 1870s. In 1871 a great fire destroyed the breweries in Chicago. Chicago's beer drinkers wanted their beer brewed by traditional German methods, so Milwaukee brewers began shipping their product to Illinois. This was a very good business move. By 1872 half of Milwaukee's beer was sold to out-of-towners. The city is still the country's leader in the beer industry.

But brewing is just one of the many German contributions to Milwaukee. Germans established theaters and musical societies, and produced German foods and crafts.

A number of famous people got their start in the area, too. Have you heard of the Ringling Brothers? As boys in Baraboo, near Milwaukee, Al and Johnny Ringling put on shows for family and friends. The brothers had a menagerie that included chickens, rabbits, a billy goat, and a horse named Zachary, which the boys had bought for just $8.42.

German brothers started *Ringling Bros. Circus*

Traditional dress at Oktoberfest

In 1882 Johnny and Al saved up $50 and took their show on the road. Johnny, who was only 14 at the time, arranged for the lots where the circus would be shown, made sure contracts were signed, and oversaw the set-up of the tents. This was a huge responsibility for such a young man, but like his brother, he was determined to succeed—and did. The Ringling Brothers called their spectacle "The Greatest Show on Earth."

37

ALBERT EINSTEIN

Almost everyone has heard of the equation, $E = mc^2$. It means that energy (E) equals mass (m) multiplied by the speed of light (c) times the speed of light. If you don't know what that means, you're not alone. When the brilliant physicist Albert Einstein came up with it, few scientists could understand it either! The equation describes the theory of relativity, which tries to explain how energy, mass, and the speed of light are related.

Einstein was born on March 14, 1879, in the town of Ulm, Germany. As a child in Munich, Albert had trouble learning his lessons in school. The teachers made students learn by rote, that is, by memorizing facts. Albert hated this method of learning.

Believe it or not, young Albert even did poorly in math and science—in school, that is. But he was a scientific genius just the same. He taught himself calculus (a complicated form of math) and was very curious about science. At 16, when other kids his age were thinking about having fun, Einstein was wondering how the universe worked.

When Einstein graduated from a technical institute in Zurich, the German-speaking part of Switzerland, he had a hard time finding a job, even as smart as he was. Finally, he heard about a position as a clerk in Berne, and he snapped it up. He could easily do the work, and in his spare time, he could think and think and think.

When Einstein published his ideas about relativity in 1905, other physicists realized he was a scientific genius. He was invited all over the world to talk about his theory. Enthusiastic crowds and heads of state greeted him as a celebrity.

When the Nazis came to power in Germany, Einstein was outraged. He spoke out against the anti-Jewish laws. And he criticized Germany for going to war again,

Young Einstein daydreaming in school

Albert Einstein's colleague Charles Steinmetz was also a genius. His field was electrical engineering. Born in Germany in 1865, he came to the U.S. at age 23. He patented more than 200 inventions that we still use today. His work on radio, television, and other electrical equipment helped General Electric in Schenectady, New York, become the major company it is today.

just a generation after World War I—which had been called "the war to end all wars." The Nazis took away Einstein's German citizenship and seized his property because he was Jewish.

In October of 1933, Einstein and his wife, Elsa, moved to the U.S. Einstein was given a position at Princeton, a highly respected university. When he wanted to concentrate on a physics problem, he would tell others, in his heavy German accent, "I will a little tink."

Throughout his life, Einstein was a pacifist (against war). But he nevertheless encouraged President Franklin D. Roosevelt to use uranium, a dangerous radioactive metal, to build an atomic bomb to end World War II. By the end of the war, Einstein was deeply troubled by the

Einstein and his famous equation

Albert Einstein (left) with Charles Steinmetz

destruction the war had caused. He wrote and lectured widely about the horrors of war in the atomic age and urged people to solve their problems peacefully. The last official paper he signed included the names of ten other famous people. It asked: "Shall we put an end to the human race; or shall mankind renounce war?"

Einstein died in Princeton, New Jersey, on April 18, 1955. He is recognized around the world as one of the greatest scientists, and humanitarians, of all time.

PROFILES OF FIVE GERMAN AMERICANS

Levi Strauss & Co. Museum

Levi Strauss (1829–1902)

Levi Strauss was born in a small village in Bavaria, in southern Germany. He crossed oceans and continents, and finally wound up in San Francisco, where he became part of the history of the American West. The work clothes he made "never wore out." For this reason, they became wildly popular with the miners who flocked to California during the gold rush. Levi Strauss & Co. is now the world's largest clothing manufacturer. Once worn only by miners, farmers, and cowboys, blue jeans are now worn by almost everyone. Maybe even you?

Margaretha Meyer Schurz (1833–1876)

Did you go to kindergarten when you were little? Margaretha Meyer Schurz studied with the founder of these classes for young children in Germany. When she moved to America with her husband Carl, the famous forty-eighter, she tried the classes here. She founded America's first kindergarten in 1856 in Watertown, Wisconsin. *Kinder* means "children" in German, and *garten* means "garden." Since then, "children gardens" have bloomed all over the country.

The Bettmann Archive

Thomas Nast (1840–1902)

At age six Thomas Nast came to America from Germany. As a teenager he got a job as an illustrator for a popular weekly magazine. During the Civil War, his pictures of the battles became famous all over the world. President Lincoln praised him for his political cartoons. Nast thought up the donkey and elephant as symbols for the Democratic and Republican parties. He was the first to draw Santa Claus as the chubby, white-bearded fellow we recognize today. His cartoon attacks on Boss Tweed, the head of a dishonest ring of politicians, helped land the crooks in jail.

Babe Ruth (1895–1948)

When George Herman Ruth was growing up, his family spoke mostly German at home. George got into trouble as a youngster, so his parents sent him to a Catholic home for orphans and delinquents. By the time he left the home a few years later, George was a hot-shot baseball player. Because he was still pretty young, his Boston Red Sox teammates called him "the babe." Babe Ruth set an American League record for shutouts in a season by a left-handed pitcher.

After joining the New York Yankees, Babe Ruth became really famous. Before Babe joined the team, they had never won a single pennant. He teamed up with Lou Gehrig, another German-American player. Over their lives, Babe Ruth and Lou Gehrig had the most runs batted in, in proportion to their times at bat. And of the ten highest slugging averages ever achieved in a season, seven are by Babe Ruth and Lou Gehrig.

Philosopher Hannah Arendt

Hannah Arendt (1904–1975)

Born in Hanover, Germany, Hannah Arendt was a very quick learner as a child. She could read before she started kindergarten. In 1929, at a time when most German women did not work outside the home, she earned the highest college degree possible. In 1933, she fled the Nazis and escaped to Paris, France. There, she worked for Jewish organizations. In 1940, she and her husband were imprisoned for six weeks by the Nazis, who had invaded France. The couple escaped to New York in 1941.

In 1951, Arendt became a U.S. citizen. That same year, she published one of her most important books. It was about the roots of brutal governments such as the Nazis'. She became recognized around the world for her political thinking and writing. She was the first woman to become a full professor at Princeton University. Throughout her life, she was a defender of hope and human dignity.

Babe Ruth autographing a baseball

41

CONTRIBUTIONS TO AMERICAN SOCIETY

American culture has been greatly enriched by its German American citizens. More Germans came to the United States than from any other country. They came to America over two centuries and settled in different parts of the country. Today, nearly 60 million people out of a total population of 248 million claim some German ancestry.

German Americans have influenced every aspect of American society. In fact, many German American contributions are so much a part of America, it's hard to see their German origins. People of German ancestry have helped to shape the very ideals and ideas that we accept as American.

Even some of our words show this influence: kindergarten, hamburgers, frankfurters, and delicatessen. And what do people sometimes say when someone sneezes? "Gesundheit," a German word.

Have you ever heard a song that reminded you of a certain person or place? Music is very powerful. For German Americans, music reminded them of the Old World after they settled in their new country. They brought with them the music of many great German composers: Bach, Mozart, Haydn, Beethoven, Schubert, Schumann, Brahms, and Wagner.

German immigrants got together to play or sing or listen to these great works. Others adapted music or wrote new works. They organized singing clubs, symphony orchestras, and other musical groups. Most musicians and directors of chamber, orchestral, and choral music in the mid-1800s in America were German. In 1890, nearly all of the 94 performers in the New York Philharmonic were German-born.

German contributions in science, tech-

National Archives

A German musical society

Which of these "American" things had a German beginning?

hamburgers	blue jeans
glee clubs	Christmas trees
Easter eggs	kindergarten
gymnastics	hot dogs
Brooklyn Bridge	symphony orchestras
Conestoga wagons	Little Red Riding Hood
skyscrapers	Ringling Bros. Circus
Republican elephant	dumplings
Democratic donkey	beer
county fairs	pretzels

Answer: All of them!

German Americans have entered and excelled in many professions

nology, and psychology were enormous. The ideas of physicist Albert Einstein and engineer Charles Steinmetz changed the whole world. Another scientist, Maria Meyer, immigrated to America in 1930. She won the Nobel Prize in physics in 1963, becoming the first woman to do so. Wernher von Braun, a German-born rocket and space expert, helped America achieve the first landing on the moon on July 21, 1969. And the famous psychologist Charlotte Bühler was born to German immigrants.

Amazing individuals achieved success in many fields. John Jacob Astor left his small village of Waldorf, Germany, for the glittering city of New York. He arrived flat broke—and went on to achieve the American dream of going from rags to riches. He built the world-famous Waldorf-Astoria Hotel and became America's first great tycoon.

John A. Roebling was another famous German immigrant. He designed the Brooklyn Bridge in New York. Ludwig Mies Van Der Rohe came from Aachen to design glassy skyscrapers and sleek-walled build-

ings. These have become prominent symbols of modern America.

Gertrude Ederle was the first woman to swim the English Channel. She beat the records of many men who had swum it before. The Flying Wallendas are a family of circus acrobats, and the Ringling Bros. produced the "Greatest Show on Earth."

Frank L. Baum was a whiz of a writer. His *Wizard of Oz* proves it. The photographer Dorothea Lange took haunting pictures of struggling families during the Great Depression. Hannah Arendt taught at leading American universities and wrote many influential books about politics.

The Bettmann Archive

Germans founded the Steinway piano factory

Children's author Dr. Seuss

organs (Wurlitzer), brewing (Pabst, Anheuser-Busch, Schlitz), language study (Berlitz), bicycles (Schwinn), glass (Steuben), food (Heinz, Kraft, Fleischmann), and even chocolate (Hershey).

Some contributions are so much a part of our lives, it's hard to imagine life without them. Music, dancing, picnics, card playing, swimming, and bowling were all introduced or promoted in the U.S. by Germans in the 1800s.

Dr. Seuss (Theodore Geisel) of *The Cat in the Hat* fame has readers all over the world. And Snoopy, Charlie Brown, Lucy, and Linus were created by the German American cartoonist Charles Schulz.

American pioneers of German ancestry influenced many industries as well: automobiles (Studebaker, Chrysler), lumber (Weyerhauser), optics (Bausch and Lomb), petroleum (Rockefeller), pianos (Steinway),

A parade of Studebaker automobiles

The famous Budweiser wagon

Have you ever joined a gymnastics class or sang in a choir? Do you belong to any clubs or organizations? Germans may have started them. They organized lodges, singing groups, orchestras, schools, theater groups, and churches.

The Midwest still shows the influence of generations of German Americans who made their living on the land. Today, many family farms are run by people who are the descendants of hardworking German American farmers.

German immigrants brought their ideas, hard work, and craftsmanship from the Old Country to the new. Their skills, thrift, perseverance, and family strength are values many Americans share. Our nation is a better place to live in because they're here.

Other books about German Americans:

Franck, Irene M. *The German-American Heritage*. New York: Facts on File, 1989.

Schwartz, Joseph and Michael McGuinness. *Einstein for Beginners*. New York: Pantheon Books, 1979.

Stoud, John Joseph. *Sunbonnets and Shoofly Pies: A Pennsylvania Dutch Cultural History*. South Brunswick & New York: A.S. Barnes & Co., 1973.

Taitz, Emily and Sondra Henry. *A Biography of Levi Strauss: Everyone Wears His Name*. Minneapolis: Dillon Press, Inc., 1990.

BIZARRE & BEAUTIFUL SERIES

A spirited and fun investigation of the mysteries of the five senses in the animal kingdom.

Each title in the series is 8½" x 11", $14.95 hardcover, with color photographs and illustrations throughout.

Bizarre & Beautiful Ears
Bizarre & Beautiful Eyes
Bizarre & Beautiful Feelers
Bizarre & Beautiful Noses
Bizarre & Beautiful Tongues

RAINBOW WARRIOR SERIES

What is a Rainbow Warrior Artist? It is a person who strives to live in harmony with the Earth and all living creatures, and who tries to better the world while living his or her life in a creative way.

Each title is written by Reavis Moore with a foreword by LeVar Burton, and is 8½" x 11", 48 pages, $14.95 hardcover, with color photographs and illustrations.

Native Artists of Africa
Native Artists of North America
Native Artists of Europe (available 9/94)

ROUGH AND READY SERIES

Learn about the men and women who settled the American West. Explore the myths and legends about these courageous individuals and learn about the environmental, cultural, and economic legacies they left to us.

Each title in the series is written by A. S. Gintzler and is 48 pages, 8½" x 11", $12.95 hardcover, with two-color illustrations and duotone archival photographs.

Available 7/94:

Rough and Ready Cowboys
Rough and Ready Homesteaders
Rough and Ready Prospectors

Rough and Ready Loggers
Rough and Ready Outlaws & Lawmen
Rough and Ready Railroaders

AMERICAN ORIGINS SERIES

Many of us are the third and fourth generation of our families to live in America. Learn what our great-great-grandparents experienced when they arrived here and how much of our lives are still intertwined with theirs.

Each title is 48 pages, 8½" x 11", $12.95 hardcover, with two-color illustrations and duotone archival photographs.

Available 6/94:

Tracing Our German Roots
Tracing Our Irish Roots
Tracing Our Italian Roots
Tracing Our Jewish Roots

Tracing Our Chinese Roots
Tracing Our Japanese Roots
Tracing Our Polish Roots

ORDERING INFORMATION
Please check your local bookstore for our books, or call 1-800-888-7504 to order direct from us. All orders are shipped via UPS; see chart below to calculate your shipping charge for U.S. destinations. **No P.O. Boxes please; we must have a street address to ensure delivery.** If the book you request is not available, we will hold your check until we can ship it. Foreign orders will be shipped surface rate unless otherwise requested; please enclose $3.00 for the first item and $1.00 for each additional item.

METHOD OF PAYMENT
Check, money order, American Express, MasterCard, or VISA. We cannot be responsible for cash sent through the mail. For credit card orders, include your card number, expiration date, and your signature, or call 1-800-888-7504. American Express card orders can be shipped only to billing address of card holder. Sorry, no C.O.D.'s. Residents of sunny New Mexico, add 6.25% tax to total.

Address all orders and inquiries to:

John Muir Publications
P.O. Box 613
Santa Fe, NM 87504

(505) 982-4078
(800) 888-7504

For U.S. Orders Totaling	Add
Up to $15.00	$4.25
$15.01 to $45.00	$5.25
$45.01 to $75.00	$6.25
$75.01 or more	$7.25

EXTREMELY WEIRD SERIES

All of the titles are written by Sarah Lovett, 8¹/₂" x 11", 48 pages, $9.95 paperbacks, with color photographs and illustrations

Extremely Weird Bats
Extremely Weird Birds
Extremely Weird Endangered Species
Extremely Weird Fishes
Extremely Weird Frogs
Extremely Weird Insects
Extremely Weird Mammals
Extremely Weird Micro Monsters
Extremely Weird Primates
Extremely Weird Reptiles
Extremely Weird Sea Creatures
Extremely Weird Snakes
Extremely Weird Spiders

X-RAY VISION SERIES

Each title in the series is 8¹/₂" x 11", 48 pages, $9.95 paperback, with color photographs and illustrations, and written by Ron Schultz.

Looking Inside the Brain
Looking Inside Cartoon Animation
Looking Inside Caves and Caverns
Looking Inside Sports Aerodynamics
Looking Inside Sunken Treasure
Looking Inside Telescopes and the Night Sky

THE KIDDING AROUND TRAVEL GUIDES

All of the titles listed below are 64 pages and $9.95 paperbacks, except for *Kidding Around the National Parks* and *Kidding Around Spain*, which are 108 pages and $12.95 paperbacks.

Kidding Around Atlanta
Kidding Around Boston, 2nd ed.
Kidding Around Chicago, 2nd ed.
Kidding Around the Hawaiian Islands
Kidding Around London
Kidding Around Los Angeles
Kidding Around the National Parks
  of the Southwest
Kidding Around New York City, 2nd ed.
Kidding Around Paris
Kidding Around Philadelphia
Kidding Around San Diego
Kidding Around San Francisco
Kidding Around Santa Fe
Kidding Around Seattle
Kidding Around Spain
Kidding Around Washington, D.C., 2nd ed.

MASTERS OF MOTION SERIES

Each title in the series is 10¹/₄" x 9", 48 pages, $9.95 paperback, with color photographs and illustrations.

How to Drive an Indy Race Car
  David Rubel
How to Fly a 747
  Tim Paulson
How to Fly the Space Shuttle
  Russell Shorto

THE KIDS EXPLORE SERIES

Each title is written by kids for kids by the Westridge Young Writers Workshop, 7" x 9", and $9.95 paperback, with photographs and illustrations by the kids.

Kids Explore America's Hispanic Heritage
112 pages

Kids Explore America's African American Heritage 128 pages

Kids Explore the Gifts of Children with Special Needs 128 pages

Kids Explore America's Japanese American Heritage 144 pages

ENVIRONMENTAL TITLES

Habitats: *Where the Wild Things Live*
Randi Hacker and Jackie Kaufman
8¹/₂" x 11", 48 pages, color illustrations, $9.95 paper

The Indian Way: *Learning to Communicate with Mother Earth*
Gary McLain
7" x 9", 114 pages, two-color illustrations, $9.95 paper

Rads, Ergs, and Cheeseburgers: *The Kids' Guide to Energy and the Environment*
Bill Yanda
7" x 9", 108 pages, two-color illustrations, $13.95 paper

The Kids' Environment Book: *What's Awry and Why*
Anne Pedersen
7" x 9", 192 pages, two-color illustrations, $13.95 paper